SPACE
DISASTERS

ANN WEIL

Air Disasters
Deadly Storms
Earthquakes
Environmental Disasters
Fires
Mountain Disasters
Sea Disasters
Space Disasters
Terrorism
Volcanoes

Development: Kent Publishing Services, Inc.
Design and Production: Signature Design Group, Inc.

SADDLEBACK PUBLISHING, INC.
Three Watson • Irvine, CA 92618-2767

Website: www.sdlback.com

Photo Credits: page 13, Stocktrek/Corbis; pages 23, 34, 35, Bettmann/Corbis; page 43, Roger Ressmyer/Corbis; page 52, KRT/NewsCom; page 60, Getty Images; page 61, Matt Stroshane/Getty Images

ISBN 1-56254-662-7

Printed in the United States of America

1 2 3 4 5 6   10 09 08 07 06

TABLE OF CONTENTS

DATAFILE

TIMELINE

April 12, 1961

Yuri Gagarin, Russian cosmonaut, is the first person to enter outer space.

July 20, 1969

Neil Armstrong is the first person to walk on the moon.

Where is Russia?

DID YOU KNOW?

The International Space Station is the largest scientific project in world history. Astronauts from different nations work together in teams of three for months at a time.

KEY TERMS

astronaut - a person who is trained to go into outer space

space station - a spacecraft that stays in space for a long time

gravity - the force that pulls objects towards the center of Earth

cosmonaut - a Russian astronaut

Chapter One:
Introduction

On July 20, 1969, astronaut Neil Armstrong stepped onto the moon. Millions of people watched this amazing event on television.

No one had ever stood on the moon before. It changed how people thought about our planet and the universe.

Now, space travel doesn't seem so extraordinary. A rocket blasting off isn't always big news anymore. Hundreds of astronauts and scientists have traveled in space.

Some people have even become space tourists. They pay a lot of money to spend a week in space. Now, people even live in space for months at a time.

Science Fiction/Science Fact

It's hard to believe that less than 50 years ago, space travel was just a fantasy. Science fiction books and movies put people in outer space. But it wasn't until 1961 that someone traveled into space.

Footprint on the surface of the moon

The first person to go into space was a Russian man named Yuri Gagarin. He orbited Earth once in a Russian rocket. Then he landed safely.

Not every space mission has gone so well. Some space accidents damage very expensive equipment. Even a minor accident can cost millions of dollars. This can be a disaster for a country's space program.

Space travel is risky. Some astronauts have died in space accidents. The total number of space-related deaths is low. But these tragedies seem much bigger. Fortunately, there are very few space disasters.

The First Space Stations

The first space stations were small laboratories that orbited Earth. Astronauts traveled to the space station in rockets. They lived and worked in space for months at a time.

There is no gravity in space. People and things are weightless. Scientists studied the effects of living in space on people and other living things. They learned a lot from experiments on these early space stations.

The Russians built the first space station. *Salyut 1* was launched on April 19, 1971. The American space station, *Skylab*, was launched two years later, in May 1973.

The Russians launched their eighth space station, *Mir*, in February, 1986. *Mir* means "peace" in Russian. Mir cosmonauts became the first people to spend more than a year in space.

There were many problems with the early space stations. Some of these turned into disasters. But the lessons learned from these catastrophes helped make the newest space station—the *International Space Station*—better and safer.

The International Space Station

Americans and Russians work with astronauts and scientists from other countries on the *International Space Station*. They do many different scientific experiments. The results of these experiments can help us learn more about life in space and life on Earth.

The *International Space Station* (ISS) orbits the Earth. Astronauts live and work on the ISS for about three to six months. Then a new crew comes to the ISS to continue the work.

The ISS is the only space station orbiting Earth. The earlier space stations are no longer in orbit.

Skylab in Trouble!

Skylab was launched on May 14, 1973.
It was more than three times larger than
Salyut 1 and weighed about 100 tons.
But only one minute after taking off,
Skylab was in serious trouble. A big
meteor shield fell off. It tore away a large
screen of solar panels. NASA launched a
team of three astronauts to fix the space
station. The astronauts fixed the problem
while *Skylab* orbited Earth.

In the International Space Station, *there are two crew cabins. Each cabin is large enough for one astronaut to sleep in.*

TIMELINE

December 3, 1967
The first successful heart transplant is performed.

January 27, 1967
A fire breaks out in the command module during practice for the Apollo 1 mission into space.

Where is the NASA launch pad? ▶▶▶▶

LAUNCH PAD

DID YOU KNOW?

In 1965, Ed White became the first American to perform the "space-walk." He floated outside the spacecraft for 23 minutes.

KEY TERMS

Soviet Union - a country that existed from 1922 to 1991 in eastern Europe. Russia was a part of the Soviet Union.

National Aeronautics and Space Administration (NASA) - an organization whose mission is to plan space activities

command module - the place where the astronauts control the spaceship

hatch - a door in the command module

Chapter Two:
Apollo 1, 1967

The United States and the Soviet Union had space programs in the 1960s. Now both countries work together on the *International Space Station*. But, in the 1960s, they did not work together. They competed against each other. Each country wanted to be the first to rule space.

At first, the Russians were ahead in the race to space. The first person in space was Russian cosmonaut Yuri Gagarin. The United States had to catch up to the Soviet Union before they could take the lead in the space race.

The Birth of NASA

American President John F. Kennedy wanted the first person on the moon to be an American. The National Aeronautics and Space Administration (NASA) was created in July 1958.

Its official mission was to plan and conduct space activities. Its real goal was to land American astronauts on the moon and return them safely to Earth.

The first two NASA projects were named Mercury and Gemini. The Mercury and Gemini projects put Americans into outer space. The third project, named Apollo, would land them on the moon.

The first Apollo spaceship was scheduled to take off on February 21, 1967. Thousands of people at NASA were working very hard to make that happen. It was supposed to be a great moment. Instead, the Apollo program began with tragedy.

A Fateful Test

On January 27, 1967, the *Apollo 1* crew was practicing for their trip into space. The crew consisted of Gus Grissom, Ed White, and Roger Chaffee. Grissom and White had both been into space before. *Apollo 1* was Chaffee's first mission in space.

The three astronauts were inside the command module of the spaceship. The command module is like the cockpit of a plane. It's where the astronauts sit to control the spaceship.

They were testing the plan for lift off. The astronauts were strapped into their seats. The command module was locked and sealed.

The astronauts could talk to the NASA team using a communications system. But the system was not working properly. NASA technicians outside the command module were trying to fix that. Everything else seemed fine.

No Escape

Then, suddenly, a fire broke out inside the command module. The astronauts reported the emergency. One of them tried to open the hatch to the outside. That was the only way to escape. But the hatch was stuck. The astronauts were trapped inside!

The flames spread quickly. The fire burned the walls of the command module. Poisonous smoke filled the inside of the command module. The fire was so hot, the command module cracked. That made a very loud noise. It sounded like an explosion.

Technicians grabbed fire extinguishers. They tried to put out the fire. But smoke from the fire made it difficult to breathe. Some of them found gas masks.

Others tried to help without gas masks. It was very difficult. There was so much smoke, they could not see. They had to open the hatches using only their sense of touch.

There were three hatches on the command module. It took almost five minutes to open them all. By then, the three astronauts were dead.

No one knows exactly when or how they died. They probably died quickly from breathing poisonous smoke. Or they might have burned to death.

The heat inside the command module was very intense. It had melted their space suits. The fire had also melted the nylon from the seats. At first, no one could move the dead bodies. They were stuck to the seats.

The Investigation

The *Apollo 1* fire was a disaster for NASA. Plans for the *Apollo 1* launch were put on hold.

There was an investigation. But the cause of the fire was never discovered. The most likely explanation was that a spark from bad electrical wiring started the fire.

The spark ignited oxygen gas inside the command module. There was a very high level of oxygen inside the command module. Oxygen burns quickly.

The tragedy was also the result of poor planning and design. Many safety changes were made following the *Apollo 1* disaster. A new fast-release escape hatch was put in the command module. The new hatch could be opened from inside in seven seconds.

The Apollo program was delayed by 21 months. But it did recover after the tragic fire. *Apollo 11* astronauts Neil Armstrong and Buzz Aldrin were the first people to walk on the moon. Five other Apollo missions also put people on the surface of the moon.

The late President Kennedy's wish was realized. And despite its tragic beginning, the Apollo program was a tremendous success.

Apollo 1 *astronauts (L-R), Virgil "Gus"*
Grissom, Edward White, and Roger Chaffee,
suited up at the Saturn launch pad.
A few days later, all three would be killed in
an electrical fire in the command module
during testing.

TIMELINE

April 11, 1970
Apollo 13 lifts off on a mission to the moon.

April 13, 1970
There is an explosion on the *Apollo 13*.

Where is the Pacific Ocean? ▶▶▶

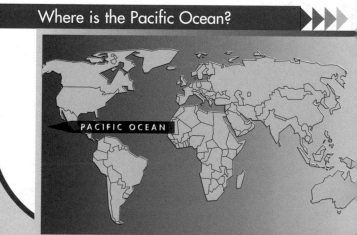

PACIFIC OCEAN

The astronauts on board *Apollo 13* ran out of water. They drank less than one cup of water each day.

KEY TERMS

German measles - a disease that causes the neck to become swollen and the skin to develop red spots

lunar module - a separate structure designed to land the astronauts on the moon

Chapter Three:
Apollo 13, 1970

The *Apollo 11* astronauts were the first people to walk on the moon. Millions of people knew the names Neil Armstrong and Buzz Aldrin.

Apollo 12 astronauts also landed on the moon. *Apollo 13* was going to be the third time American astronauts walked on the moon.

But *Apollo 13* never landed on the moon. Two days after it took off from Earth, *Apollo 13* was in trouble. A tank of oxygen exploded.

The blast damaged the spacecraft. It looked as though the astronauts would not be able to return to Earth. They might be stranded in space!

Unlucky 13?

Some people believe the number 13 is unlucky. The explosion on *Apollo 13* happened on the 13th of April. But the mission's bad luck began even before the spacecraft took off.

Three days before launch, there was a last-minute crew change. The *Apollo 13* crew was accidentally exposed to German measles.

Two of the crew had already had the disease. They could not get it again. But the command module pilot had never had German measles.

NASA doctors were afraid he would get sick during the mission. They would not let him go on the mission. The back-up pilot, Jack Swigert, replaced him.

Swigert was an experienced pilot. But he had not been training with the other two crew members. Space missions depend on excellent teamwork. The three astronauts had to learn how to work together. And they had only two days to get used to each other.

Three…two…one…lift off!

Apollo 13 lifted off on April 11, 1970. At first everything went well. All systems were working properly.

On their third day in space, the astronauts made a TV broadcast. They showed how they lived and worked in space. People back on Earth could see what it was like to be weightless.

But less than ten minutes after they finished this, something went very wrong.

There was a sharp bang. The spaceship shook. Warning lights in the command module showed that two of the three fuel supplies were gone. The fuel provided electricity for everything on the spacecraft.

The astronauts quickly realized they would not be able to land on the moon. There wasn't enough power left. They were terribly disappointed.

Then they saw that their oxygen supplies were dangerously low. One of the astronauts looked out the window. He saw the oxygen gas spraying out of the spacecraft.

This was much more serious than not landing on the moon. They needed this oxygen to breathe. Without it, they would die. And without power, the spacecraft would not be able to get them home.

The three astronauts realized that making it back to Earth alive would be a miracle.

No Air, No Water, No Power

The astronauts lost most of their oxygen within three hours. They also lost their water.

There was almost no power left. The command module was supposed to be the astronaut's control center in space. Now it was useless.

But the lunar module was still attached. This was the astronauts' only hope. They moved into the lunar module. It became their lifeboat in space.

Lunar Module Lifeboat

The lunar module had its own supply of oxygen. It also had a separate power supply.

The explosion had not affected the lunar module. It still had oxygen and power. But would it be enough to keep the astronauts alive till they could return safely to Earth?

The lunar module was designed to land two astronauts on the moon. After two days on the moon, the two astronauts would return to the command module. The third astronaut would remain in the command module.

Now all three astronauts needed to live in the lunar module. It would take them four days to get back to Earth.

The lunar module was not designed to support three astronauts for four days. Still, it was the only way the astronauts could survive their trip back to Earth. They had to make it work.

Struggle for Survival

The astronauts had enough oxygen to breathe. They circled the moon. Then they used the power left in the lunar module to push themselves back toward Earth.

They were on their way home. But there was very little water. Each astronaut drank less than a cup of water a day. That was less than a fifth of what they were supposed to drink.

There was no power to heat the spacecraft. The astronauts were freezing cold.

There was no hot water to put in their food either. Space food is usually dehydrated. Normally the astronauts would add hot water to the food, then eat it. But without hot water, the food was useless. The astronauts ate very little.

It was a long, cold, hungry four days. But the astronauts returned safely to Earth on April 17. They splashed down into the Pacific Ocean. They were tired, hungry, and thirsty. One of the astronauts had lost 14 pounds. But they were alive, and very happy to be home.

A Successful Failure?

The *Apollo 13* mission did not land on the moon. It was a $375 million failure. But everyone was very relieved the three astronauts were safe. Getting them home alive under the circumstances was a tremendous achievement.

Navy swimmers fasten a floatation collar around the Apollo 13 *capsule as it floats after splashdown in the Pacific Ocean.*

34

Left to right: Fred Haise, lunar module pilot; James Lovell, commander; and Jack Swigert, command module pilot, wave to a crowd after their successful splashdown.

TIMELINE

April 19, 1971

Salyut 1, the world's first space station, is launched.

April 23, 1971

The first space station crew leaves for Salyut 1.

Where was the Soviet Union?

DID YOU KNOW?

Vladimir M. Komarov was the first person to die in a space mission, in 1967. While returning to Earth, the main parachute did not open. The rocket crashed into the ground.

KEY TERMS

valve - a device that controls the flow of a gas

suffocate - to stop a person from breathing

space suit - a special suit that allows astronauts to survive in space

Chapter Four:
Soyuz 11, 1971

The Russians knew they could not win the moon race. Instead, they focused on building the first space station. They launched *Salyut 1* in April 1971.

Salyut 1 was the world's first space station. *Salyut* means "salute" in Russian. The name was chosen in memory of cosmonaut Yuri Gagarin. Gagarin was the first person in space. He was a Russian hero. In 1968, Gagarin was killed in a plane crash.

Soyuz

The *Salyut 1* space station was launched without anyone inside. Cosmonauts traveled to the space station on a small rocket ship called *Soyuz*. *Soyuz* means "union" in Russian. These rockets could make one trip up into space and back. A new Soyuz rocket was used for each trip.

The first crew arrived at *Salyut 1* four days after the space station was launched. But they did not get inside. They could not open the hatch. They came back to Earth without entering the space station.

The second crew did get into the space station. This was the first time a space station was occupied. The three cosmonauts stayed on *Salyut 1* for 23 days. That was the longest anyone had ever been in space. The Russians were very proud of this achievement.

Space Science

Space stations are like small laboratories. The cosmonauts did experiments. They wanted to see how people reacted to being in space for long periods of time.

They studied themselves to find out how their bodies reacted to being weightless. They also studied Earth's weather. The information they gathered would help improve weather forecasts.

The cosmonauts completed their experiments. It was time for them to leave the space station. They boarded their Soyuz rocket.

The rocket separated from the space station. It orbited Earth three times. The cosmonauts were ready to come back to Earth.

It seemed like their mission was a

complete success. But disaster was about to strike. The three men would not make it back to Earth alive.

Dead on Arrival

Mission Control tried to contact the cosmonauts as they returned to Earth. But there was no answer. Still, everything seemed all right.

Soyuz rockets were programmed to return to Earth. The crew did not have to pilot the rocket back to Earth.

The *Soyuz 11* landed on schedule. The ground crew opened the hatch. They were ready to welcome the three heroes home.

But instead they had a horrible shock. The three men were dead. They had died in space.

At first, these deaths were a mystery.

No one knew what had happened. The cosmonauts were found still strapped in their seats. There were no signs that they had tried to get out.

One idea was that they had all suffered heart attacks. But that was not what happened. The tragedy was caused by a fault in the rocket.

A valve opened by accident. The air inside the rocket rushed out. The three men suffocated to death.

If they had been wearing space suits, they would have survived. But the *Soyuz 11* was very small. The three cosmonauts were squeezed inside.

There was not enough room for them to wear space suits. They relied on air inside the rocket to breathe. But when the valve opened, all the air escaped. They could not breathe, so they died.

This disaster delayed the Soviet space program. The Soviet Union did not send a new crew to *Salyut 1*. Two years passed before they sent any more cosmonauts into space. And from then on, all cosmonauts wore spacesuits for launch and landing.

Launch of a Soyuz Mission, June 24, 1982

TIMELINE

April 12, 1981
The first space shuttle, *Columbia*, is launched.

January 28, 1986
The *Challenger* space shuttle explodes less than two minutes after lift off.

Where is New Hampshire?

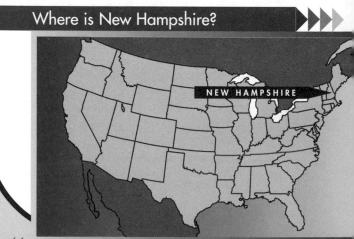

NEW HAMPSHIRE

DID YOU KNOW?

It takes a space shuttle about ten minutes to get into its low orbit at 115 miles above Earth.

KEY TERMS

space shuttle - a reusable spacecraft that lifts off like a rocket and lands like an airplane

Teacher in Space Program (TISP) - a NASA program designed to give teachers a chance to go into space

ground - to stop

seal - a cap placed over the lid of a container

Chapter Five:
Challenger, 1986

The American space shuttle takes off like a rocket. It orbits the Earth like a spacecraft. And it lands like an airplane.

NASA started the space shuttle program in the 1970s. They wanted a spacecraft that could carry heavy loads into space. They also wanted this new spacecraft to be reusable.

Previous spacecraft could be used only once. These early American and Russian rockets could make only one trip into space and back.

The same space shuttle can be used again and again. It can also carry very large, heavy objects. It brings satellites and parts of the *International Space Station* up into space to orbit Earth.

The first space shuttle, *Columbia*, lifted off on April 12, 1981. Since then, there have been more than a hundred successful space shuttle missions. But the most famous space shuttle mission was a disaster.

Space Shuttle *Challenger*

Challenger was NASA's second space shuttle. It started flying in 1982. It successfully completed nine missions.

Challenger's tenth mission was the 25th space shuttle flight. *Challenger* was originally scheduled to lift off January 22, 1986. But there were many delays.

Bad weather and strong winds were partly to blame. There were also problems with the space shuttle itself. Part of the hatch had to be sawed off when it could not be removed any other way. There were other problems, too. One of the fire monitors was not working properly.

Finally, almost a week late, *Challenger* lifted off. But its flight would last less than two minutes and end in tragedy.

A Teacher in Space

Usually only NASA astronauts and scientists go up on the space shuttle. But the tenth *Challenger* mission was special. It was the first flight of a new NASA program called the Teacher in Space Program (TISP).

The *Challenger* was scheduled to carry Sharon Christa McAuliffe, the first teacher to fly in space. Christa McAuliffe was a high school teacher from New Hampshire. She was going to teach lessons from space to students around the country.

More than 11,000 teachers applied to TISP. They all wanted to go up on the space shuttle. McAuliffe trained for many months before the flight.

She was very excited about the opportunity to be part of the space program. Her students were very proud of their teacher.

The lift off was broadcast live. TVs were turned on in schools all over the country so children could watch the *Challenger* lift off as it happened. They watched the *Challenger* lift off. And they saw it destroyed in a puff of smoke.

Challenger blew apart 73 seconds after it took off. The space shuttle and its seven-person crew were lost.

Millions of people watched this disaster as it happened on television. It was a horrible shock. It left America, and the world, stunned and sad.

A Terrible Loss

NASA had never lost an astronaut in flight. Now it lost an entire seven-person crew.

The entire space shuttle program was grounded. NASA had to figure out what went wrong. They needed to make sure the same thing wouldn't happen to the other space shuttles.

They looked closely at pictures of the *Challenger* blasting off. There was a puff of smoke coming from one of the rocket boosters less than a second after take off.

Computer images confirmed there was a problem with one of the solid rocket booster seals. Hot gas leaked out. This started a fire. The fire caused the fuel to explode within the rocket, which destroyed the space shuttle.

New Safety Plans

NASA made many changes after the *Challenger* disaster. They fixed the seals in the other space shuttles. New, stricter safety plans were put into effect.

NASA built a new space shuttle in 1991. The *Endeavour* replaced *Challenger*. Once again, NASA had a fleet of four space shuttles.

Space shuttle Challenger *exploding in flight*

TIMELINE

February 1, 2003
Columbia explodes as it returns to Earth.

April 16, 2003
Columbia Space Shuttle Program Director,
Ron Dittemore, decides to leave his job.
He was director for 26 years.

Where is Texas?   ▶▶▶

TEXAS

DID YOU KNOW?

After the *Columbia* exploded, NASA planned a 555,000-acre search in Texas and Louisiana. The searchers looked for pieces of the shuttle on land, sea, and even in the air.

KEY TERMS

bail out - to escape

parachute - a piece of material that opens like an umbrella to give a person a safe landing

experiment - a scientific test

Chapter Six:
Columbia, 2003

The second shuttle disaster happened in February 2003. Space shuttle *Columbia* blew apart as it was returning to Earth.

The Crew

Seven astronauts were on board Columbia when it exploded. Six were Americans. Rick Husband was the commander. William McCool was the pilot. The other American astronauts were Kalpana Chawla, Michael Anderson, David Brown, and Laurel Clark. The seventh astronaut was from Israel. His name was Ilan Ramon. Ramon was a colonel in the Israeli Air Force. This was the first time an Israeli astronaut had gone into space.

Only three of the *Columbia* astronauts had been in space before. It was the first trip for Brown, Clark, McCool , and Ramon.

Astronauts wear special suits when they return to Earth. These suits have a parachute. But *Columbia* blew apart so quickly there was no time for the crew to bail out.

Small Holes, Big Trouble

This disaster happened just 16 minutes before *Columbia* was supposed to land. The outside of the space shuttle gets very, very hot as it comes down to Earth. Special tiles protect the space shuttle and the astronauts from this heat. But this time, something went wrong. Super hot gas got inside the left wing of the shuttle. This caused the shuttle to blow apart.

NASA wanted to know what caused these small holes. There were several possibilities. During lift-off, a piece of foam broke off and hit the wing. This may have damaged tiles that protect the shuttle when it comes back to Earth. Or maybe something else hit the shuttle and made a hole.

Columbia's 28th Mission

The *Columbia* astronauts were almost home when their mission turned to tragedy. They had been in space for 16 days. Some astronauts are also scientists. Their job is to complete experiments in space. Many of these focus on how the human body reacts to being in space. On this mission, astronauts were studying why people lose bone and muscle when they stay in space.

They also studied spiders. Students in Australia had prepared that experiment. They were testing whether spiders can spin webs in zero gravity.

Picking up the Pieces

Some people on the ground heard a loud boom when the *Columbia* exploded. They saw pieces of the space shuttle fall to the ground. Luckily, no one was hurt by the falling pieces.

Pieces from the space shuttle were scattered over a very large area. Thousands of police, soldiers, and volunteers collected as many as they could find. NASA hopes that studying what's left of the shuttle will help them answer more questions about what happened.

The crew of the space shuttle Columbia *walk onto the launch pad. In the first row, pilot William McCool (left) and commander Rick Husband (right). In the second row are mission specialists Kalpana Chawla (left) and Laurel Clark (right). In the last row, payload specialist Ilan Ramon, payload commander Michael Anderson and mission specialist David Brown. Ilan Ramon was the first Israeli astronaut to travel into space.*

Columbia *was the first space shuttle. Its first trip into space was in 1981. Here the shuttle* Columbia *lifts off for its last mission on January 16, 2003. The* Columbia *was lost when it broke up upon re-entry to Earth on February 1, 2003. The disaster happened at the end of* Columbia*'s 28th trip.*

Epilogue

After the *Challenger* exploded, Christa McAuliffe's back-up kept working with NASA. Her name is Barbara Morgan. She was a teacher from Idaho. Morgan traveled across the country. She talked with teachers and students about her time with NASA. Now Barbara Morgan is a full-time astronaut.

In 2003, NASA formed the Educator Astronaut Program. Educator Astronauts talk with students while they are in space. The Internet and videos are two ways they do this. Students can tell NASA about a teacher they think would be a good Educator Astronaut.

You can support the Educator Astronauts by going online and joining the Earth Crew. The Earth Crew completes missions here on Earth.

Bibliography

Bredeson, Carmen. *The Challenger Disaster: Tragic Space Flight.* American Disasters. Springfield, NJ: Enslow Publishers, 1999.

Brubaker, Paul. *Apollo 1 Tragedy: Fire in the Capsule.* American Disasters. Berkeley Heights, NJ: Enslow Publishers, 2002.

Landau, Elaine. *Space Disasters.* Watts Library. New York: Franklin Watts, 1999.

Stott, Carole. *Space Exploration.* Eyewitness Books. New York: Dorling Kindersley, 2000.

Vogt, Gregory. *Disasters in Space Exploration.* Brookfield, CT: Millbrook Press, 2001.

Index